FROM BURNING BLOCKS TO BUILDING BLOCKS

FROM BURNING BLOCKS TO BUILDING BLOCKS

WILLIAM LICEA

From Burning Blocks to Building Blocks

SYG Publishing
Congers, New York

LCCN: 2022918934

Print ISBN: 979-8-9871234-0-9
Hardcover ISBN: 979-8-9871234-1-6

Ebook ISBN: 979-8-9871234-2-3

TABLE OF CONTENTS

ACKNOWLEDGMENTS

FIRST AND FOREMOST I would like to thank God, even when I was doing wrong I felt your presence.

My mother and father, Miriam & Eleugerio Licea, who are in heaven watching over me. I shine for you!

My wife and daughter, Aracelis & Ocean Licea. Thank you for always urging me to follow my dreams. I love you.

My sisters, Glenda and Gretel, I love you guys. Thank you for helping to raise me, you were my motivation.

My nieces, nephews and brother-in-laws. I love you all.

My nephew Glen, Mia and Jen. Glen, thank you for truly listening to what I said; because of you connecting me with Peter, this book is now real. Also, thank you for holding me down while I was in prison all those years and when I needed a helping hand out here.

My wife's parents: Juana Laureano (RIP) we are still feeling your loss and you will always be missed. Jose-Luis, thank you for being there for us. We love you.

My wife's siblings, Janet, Juan, Irving, Nilsa, Brenda, Elaine, thank you guys for accepting me into the family. Jeffrey, we are proud of you for being a Marine. We look up to you, thank you for serving our country.

G, Danny and Garry (RIP). Thank you for making the connection and helping me land my first job ever.

Mike Falco, President of Defalco Construction: without your guidance, tutelage and the special interest that you took in me, none of this would be possible. From day one, I followed your lead and now I have hundreds of men that follow me and for that I will always be indebted to you.

All Defalco personnel, office and field team Avi, Joe, Modesto, Davie, Juan, and Mark Dbest, thank you all!

To all my friends in and out of prison, to all that have stayed the path, much respect, Ed (Madball), Wolfie, we see you! I know it's not an easy road. To all friends that have not followed or stayed the path, I will always be rooting for you. Those still fighting for freedom, my heart goes out to all of you.

Peter Lopez and the book team. Thank you.

Sasha, I look forward to more ventures with you. Thank you.

Willie Falcon: I learned a lot from you, for five years I was taking notes. Thank you for helping me and mine when we needed it the most.

INTRODUCTION

THE ODDS MAKERS will put it to you this way.

If you ever make it out of prison, there's a seventy-six percent chance you'll end up back in the yard within the first five years of your release.

That would be three out of every four freed inmates returning to prison within the first year of their release. In other words, the odds are stacked against you. Heavily. I can share stories of more than a few who couldn't survive their so-called freedom.

But there's different types of freedoms, aren't there? Different types of environments. The streets where I come from were never an easy place to survive.

We're talking the 80's in the South Bronx. Gangs, guns, drugs, violence. Those were my streets, where I lived a life that would eventually put me in prison for nearly two decades, burning the prime years of my life.

I left prison when I was thirty-eight years old, with very few life skills to help me as a free man. I'll put it to you like this; the last time I went to school was in the eight grade, in which I decided on a different type of education, if you want to say that.

A street education. It started with petty crime and escalated from there. I guess you could call the first time I threw a brick through a car window and blew the thing up, my high school degree, my first juvenile sentence, the equivalent of my bachelors.

My masters degree was a nine year sentence with the state, and my hard earned PhD would be my ten year stint with the Feds.

That's the life I lived and dedicated myself to with everything I had. I went all in, early. We're talking twelve, thirteen years of age. I was just a kid.

I grew up in the streets as a criminal, hustler and thug, and I was raised in the prisons. That was my life. That's all I knew.

At the age of thirty-eight I was released with no skills, very few legitimate connections, and from the outside looking in, it would seem, very little hope. But I did not become a statistic. Despite everything that was against me and despite the terrible things I had done and had done to me, I beat the odds. I passed my first year out, and never went back.

Not only that. In only twelve years since my release, I have built a life and family that I never dreamed was possible.

I tell you this because although I had everything stacked against me, I found my way. And the truth is if I did, I truly believe it's possible for you to find your way as well. No matter what you're up against, no matter what you've done or who you are, you can always turn things around. My life is proof of that.

There's a reason why most don't make it, I know. I was there. As you'll find out throughout my story, I was nearly pulled back into the life I was trying desperately to flee. With few life skills to offer society, you're spit out onto the streets to somehow make your way. And if those streets are anything like the South Bronx, you don't have to look far to be tempted by your past, including the people in it.

But I had the will, I guess my parents got my name right. That's what you need the most. Not just the will to stay out of prison, but the will to find a way and make a better life.

The thing is, I can't give you that will, you have to find it inside yourself. I hope this book and my story helps you do that.

As I kept telling myself throughout my hardest moment, and continue to tell myself: Give yourself a chance.

No matter the situation, Give yourself a chance.

Give yourself a chance.

If you repeat it enough, the chance you've given yourself can turn everything around. That's the truth, so help me God.

I gave myself a chance. Now it's your turn.

CHAPTER ONE

I DIDN'T GRADUATE HIGH school, at least not in the traditional sense. As in going into a building with other kids my age, in order to sit still in a crowded classroom, open books, listen to a teacher speak, do assignments, take tests and so on.

When I think about high school, my adolescent years where instead of being in a classroom, I was in the streets creating havoc or looking for the next opportunity to do so is what comes to mind. It's often said that habits are what make you who you are. Habits, those things you do over and over. Day after day.

By the time I was eighteen, hanging out on Union Avenue with our crew was a habit. One day Julian showed up all jacked, saying he'd been watching this kid by Longwood Ave, and that this kid was "moving some serious weight." I had already been in and out of various prisons and juvenile detention centers, and arrested more times than I care to count. And it was for good reason. Let's just say my daily habits lead me there, those activities of which you are about to read a lot more of. Before I get into the action of that day in 1992 that would put me behind bars for years to come, I want you to know one important thing. I am no longer the same person as the one you're going to learn about. It took many years, but I eventually changed from the kid I was. I had to, because my destiny was not to rot in a prison for the rest of my life. My destiny was to turn things around, write this book, and let others know they could do the same.

The change wasn't easy. Life would have to get a lot worse for me to question my own choices, to face what I had done. Because I was completely immersed in the energies of the streets.

Julian spoke the word, and we were already on route. It didn't take much, just the possibility of taking down a dealer got me going.

Pedro, another one in our crew, tagged along. As we crossed 156th St. Julian explained he'd been watching the dealer enough to be able to predict his movements—he would work his corner then go back to his building where he lived.

We walked along Longwood until we spotted him working his hustle. He looked to be in his early twenties, a light skinned Spanish guy, like me. We stayed far enough back in the park on the corner, lurking in the shadows, watching the bundles change hands. Nothing new for this neighborhood. Dealers and druggies were part of the everyday scenery.

We were patient, waiting. Eventually it was time for him to re-up, and that was our cue. He moved past us, and didn't take special notice.

We followed him to the front of his building and into the courtyard. He opened the gate to get in as we slid in right behind him into the hallway. By the time he knew he had company, there were three guns pointed at his face.

The pros that we were, we knew the drill, and what to do and say.

"Open the door. We know what you got."

As expected he tried the denial game, playing innocent.

"I don't have nothing." I could see he was scared but doing his best to hide his fear, until...

"You either open the door, or we'll kill you," I said.

"Okay, don't kill me, please don't kill me."

He turned surprisingly desperate and that's when I knew we could get him for everything.

"Then open the damn door!"

So he did. And we blew in there and searched the place. When all was said and done we had about two thousand in cash, five thousand in drugs, and some jewelry.

"If you got problems, you know us, you know where we're at," I said to him as we left the apartment. Man, was I arrogant.

As soon as we were back in our hood, we hid the guns and stashed the drugs. As for the jewelry, we were already wearing it. That kind of thing, especially the chains, were a status symbol where we were from, a way to show your manhood. I guess when you don't have much else, you need to show the world you have some worth and that was our way of doing it.

Not even a half hour later, as we're hanging out enjoying the spoils of our last misguided takedown, the cops show up in full force and surround us.

"Freeze. Don't move."

We knew this drill, too. On the streets, the power gets flipped, quick. Now we were on the other end of someone else's gun.

"This guy's claiming that you took his jewelry," one of the cops said. He was a neighborhood guy who's stopped us before. In fact, we had run-ins with all the cops present.

I spotted the rat. He was sitting nice and tight in the back of one of the cruisers. He must have been really enjoying what he saw.

"I don't know what you're talking about," I said.

They threw us up against the wall, reading our Miranda rights. Then patted us down and found cash and jewelry.

I concocted a defense: "He pawned this shit to us. He's lying, he just wants it back."

But then they found one of our guns, which was hidden by a tree. That definitely didn't work in our favor.

I explained that the money was ours as well. Despite my best attempt to get us out of the situation, we were taken to the 41st. precinct and booked. Let's just say this wasn't my first time being arrested, but it was the first time I was sent to an adult prison: The Bronx house detention center. On the corner of 161st street the place was old, and looked like a big haunted house. Pedro and I were thrown into one big dorm style room with fifty or sixty other men. At some point Pedro turned to me and asked a question that would define all those years I spent in prison:

"In here you're either a wolf or a sheep. Which do you choose, Will?"

It's the kind of question you answer for yourself first. Then, your actions prove what you've told yourself. And in this sort of environment, there is very little room for the social nuances of the outside world. This was made clear on our second day in the Bronx house.

Pedro and I were in there, waiting to use the phone. Imagine, they've only got one phone for fifty men. As the law goes, you have the right to a six minute call every day. But that's paper law, and inside prison, you've got the law of the jungle.

In theory, the COs (corrections officers) are supposed to manage the phones, giving each inmate his allotted time. But that's not how it works in reality. Instead, they allow the inmates to police it. So when it's our turn the dude running the phones told us we each had six minutes. Pedro being Pedro, said he didn't do the six minute thing. So the dude asked how long we were going to be. A reasonable question.

"Whenever we're done," Pedro spat out, his whole attitude showing arrogance and contempt at the same time.

So Pedro made his call, and when he was done passed it on to me. So far no issues. It was when I was done with my call and Pedro took back the phone that the guy jumped back in to intervene and that was when, phone in hand, Pedro caught him clean across the face.

Now the adrenaline was flowing. We were making a movie with us in the starring roles. Those roles called for us to make sure we held our status as wolves. Top of the food chain.

This is not to say that I'm proud of who we were or what we did. My point is not the glorification of my life on the streets or in the prison system. Actually, it's the complete opposite. Till this day it hurts me to think of who I was and the kind of life I lived. I let down everyone; my mother, my father, and myself. At the time I was caught up in the mania of the street life, which meant taking your survival into your own hands. That was just the way it was. Especially inside those prison walls.

From the Bronx house I was sent to Riker's Island. Riker's isn't just one prison as people from the outside assume, but a network of prison complexes located on a small island in the East River between Queens and the Bronx, with only one bridge connecting it to the main-land, to Astoria Heights in Queens.

I spent close to a year at The Beacon, one of the newer buildings that actually had air conditioning and what I later realized was a luxury. We spent time in our cells and were also given time to watch TV in the main common area. From there I was moved to the House Detention for Men (HDM), which was old, and had three floors with forty cells per tier, the kind of scene you see in movies. A few years before I got to HDM, an inmate was stabbed on the third floor, and pushed off the railing to his death. Since then, they closed off the third floor, fearing a repeat.

This was definitely not the Beacon prison. I remember transferring there in the summer of 1993. It was hot, there was no A/C. Again, life was funneled down to power struggles, a lot of it playing out over the phones.

At HDM there were four phones, two for the Blacks, two for the Spanish, as anyone of Latin descent was called. It was all about getting phone time, and holding it during the prime hours. Even though it was the COs job to organize phone time, the reality was all they did was count the prisoners to make sure everyone was accounted for. Other than that, it was the prisoners that laid down the law of the land. That meant we had to fend for ourselves. What ended up happening was that prisoners aligned across two main racial groups; Blacks and Spanish. Just like on the streets, powerful gangs grew out of those groups, the two biggest rivals being the Latin Lions and the Brotherhood. At that time the Latin Lions and Spanish gangs as a whole controlled New York, both inside the prison walls, and on the street. However, the Brotherhood was growing and would soon prove to be just as savage and crazy as we were, if not worse.

Another thing that stood out for me during those early days at HDM was the relationship between the COs and us prisoners. Sometimes you had to wonder who was worse. Like when I saw an inmate sniffing coke off a magazine. The guy offered me some but when I saw the CO approaching, I yelled at him, “Yo put that away. Put that away!”

“What’s up with you?” he said, keeping his calm. The CO caught on, said, “Out on the streets you weren’t afraid of the law and now in here you are?” He couldn’t care less what we did. That’s when I realized the prisons were just as bad as the streets. In case it’s unclear, I hadn’t even been charged with a crime yet. As far as the law was concerned, I was still innocent. I would have to spend nearly two years in this hell hole before even going to trial.

6 12

CHAPTER TWO

BY THE TIME my trial approached I had made my bones. As far as the inmate hierarchy was concerned, I was known and respected. I also did my best to keep the peace. I was even able to maintain harmony with the phones, which is a bigger deal than you can imagine.

This may sound strange to you considering my background, but I never sought out conflict for the sake of it. Whenever the opportunity arose, I did my best to avoid unnecessary conflict. I knew how to talk, make compromises, work the system and those who held the power. That's exactly what I had set up at HDM. After all, when you're in it to survive, you have to use more than fists and knives. But not everyone thinks like that, not even your allies. Case in point was my man Little D.

One day Little D came in and ruined all the work I had done on the harmony front by getting into a fight with some guy from the Brotherhood over, yes, the phones. Part of the unwritten prison code is when one of yours gets into a fight, you back him up. So, the next thing I knew, Little D and I were in an all-out brawl. Which meant the ERU, Emergency Riot Unit, was sent in and we got thrown to the cold, hard floor and handcuffed. We called these guys the Ninja Turtles, because they entered the scene all suited up with heavy protection including full knee pads, helmets, shields, and goggles. Their tactical weapons include tear gas, pepper spray, and batons in order to neutralize anything from a rebellious inmate to stop a full-on riot. Once they arrive, things get sorted out fast.

The final outcome? I get sent to the box. Which meant that I would begin my trial while serving a 120-day sentence in solitary confinement.

During the lead up to trial my lawyer suggested taking a plea deal or testifying against my co-defendants, Pedro and Julian. I refused both outright. First, I would never rat on a friend, period. It was another one of the codes of the streets, our version of the Ten Commandments.

Commandment #1: Never rat on a friend. In our world there was a special place in hell for rats. Even the name spells it out. Rat—a rodent, a parasite, a dirty, despicable creature.

There's even more to say about rats during my time at Riker's, but of the animal kind.

When my trial came around, I was shuttled from the prison to the Bronx Supreme Courthouse. Sometimes I was out for twelve hours or more and was fed a banana with a mini box of cereal in the morning, and a bologna sandwich for lunch. When I got back to my cell I was always starving, and my dinner food tray would be out waiting for me. The problem was sometimes it was left on the cell floor for so long that the roaches and rats got into it. Disgusting as it sounds, I often devoured the food even after those vile creatures nibbled on it.

As for taking a plea deal, I honestly never thought the case would get to trial, as the person we were charged with robbing was a known drug dealer. I was very surprised when he was able to take the witness stand and testify against us. Not only did he get up there to testify, but so did his girlfriend, who I never remember being in the apartment when we burst in. But I guess when your number's up, your number's up. The trial lasted two weeks. We were found guilty on all counts. I was sentenced to nine to eighteen years, while Pedro, being older and having a previous adult record got fifteen to life. As for Julian, who originally hatched the plan, his case was dismissed because the drug dealer couldn't identify him. Ironic, isn't it? Surely not a case of justice served. When the judge asked if I had any final words regarding my case, I said that despite the verdict and the sentence, I maintained my innocence.

Once that was done, Pedro and I were given a moment in private together in the bullpen, the cages that held us in another room, and we both shed a tear. After all, these were not one- or two-year sentences. We were preparing ourselves for the long haul and everything that came with it. This was our field of endeavor, and we vowed to get through it. Most of all, we pledged to each other that no matter what happened we would stay tough and always keep it real.

On June 1st, 1994, at the age of twenty, I was sent to begin my time in Downstate Correctional Facility, a maximum-security prison north of the city between New York and Albany, just east of the Hudson River. Once I was received and it came time for my run down, things became very real, very fast. Up until this point, I had been in Riker's, held there for almost two years awaiting trial. It's still appalling to me that most of us at

Riker's were pre-trial inmates, meaning we were not yet charged with a crime. Two years is a long time to wait in limbo. But all that was over now.

They took me through the threshold. It was a twilight zone moment. I walked through a door and it boomed close with a hollow echo. I was now face to face with a big white CO, nothing like I had seen at Riker's. He told me to strip down. I started the process, which made the twilight zone moment that much more extreme. To strip down in a public place is one thing, say in a gym or pool. In those places there may be other people around, but they aren't necessarily focused on you. Now replace those people, with one person, the most intimidating, hostile face you can find. Think now, he's staring at you as you strip, and while you do so, he recites the rules in this screwed up kingdom you've just entered. And then comes the worst part—butt naked, he tells me to turn around and yes, you guessed it, to spread my cheeks. Not the cute kind.

"This is a whole other world," the man began saying. "You're no longer mingling with your New York COs at Riker's. This here is God's land. If you follow the rules, you'll be alright. Otherwise, you will feel every last bit of God's wrath come down on you... do you understand?"

Next, you're told to shower and sprayed down with disinfectant, as if you're some kind of insect, like a roach. I probably was nothing more than a creature to them. I was handed a green uniform, and then came the last part, the last bit to help dismantle my identity—they put me in a chair and shaved my head clean. Like in the military.

Once my uniform was on I noticed there was a number sewn onto the shirt pocket, a number I will never forget: 94A3818.

That's right, I had gone from being Cuban Will, the big wild dog running the street, a number one gangster in one of the most feared gangs in the South Bronx, and now I was just a number. I didn't feel sorry for myself though, I never have. Playing the victim has never been part of my DNA. This attitude helped me survive in prison, and it especially helped later on in life as I needed every ounce of courage and character to free myself from the life that I had invested so many years in. In the early days of my sentence, an old timer told me, "Look sympathy up in the dictionary. It's somewhere in there between shit and suicide."

Sure, in the moment it burned. It was a drug dealer's testimony that sealed the deal and led to my long prison sentence. Still, I always took accountability for my part of the equation. I did shove a gun into the guy's face and rob him, and I knew despite who he was, why the government and the cops made deals with people like him. It was because of people like me.

They needed someone's cooperation even if that person was hardly an angel, and probably had plans to eventually nail that guy as well. Overall, I accepted my sentence and treatment because it was the result of the choices I made. Pure and simple.

I was the architect, and the prisons where I ended up were a result of my own building, brick by brick, by my own hands. There was never a question about that.

CHAPTER THREE

I STARTED FIGHTING EARLY. Being the only Cuban in the South Bronx among Blacks, Puerto Ricans, and Dominicans meant I was always the one that stuck out. That's not to say I ever tried to fit in or pretend I was anything other than who I was. I was unapologetically Cuban, and proud. My parents made sure of it. From a young age my heritage was ingrained in me by my parents who were originally from Cuba.

Both my parents were born and raised in Cuba. My father, Eleugerio Licea, was an intense, serious man, twenty years older than my mother. By the time he met my mother, he was already a father of seven. He had two daughters with my mother while living in Cuba, Glenda and Gretel, before having to flee the island because of the revolution. Like many who fled to the US, my father was pro Bautista, which meant that when Fidel Castro got ahold of the reins of power, it was time to high tail it out. When my second sister Gretel was born in 1968, my father was in Spain, where he spent two years before coming to New York. It wasn't until 1971, when he brought my mother and sisters to New York from Cuba that they were all reunited. By that time, my father was already working as a porter in a high rise building in Manhattan. When my mother arrived she wasted no time and went straight to work, getting a job at the same company.

I came into this world two years later, 1973. Born in Harlem, I was the only one in the family born an American. Since my parents worked nights, I was often left in the care of my sister Glenda, who was thirteen years older. Over time she became like a second mother to me. I was so attached to Glenda that once when she was twenty and I was seven, my parents kicked her out of the house and I actually left the house with her, and spent a week at her friend's place. My relationship with my sister couldn't account for the fighter spirit in me, which lasted years beyond me being in her care. Maybe it was passed on from my father who was a tough guy, an ex-boxer. One of his jobs in Cuba was working as a bodyguard. Or perhaps my fighting ways had less to do with genes or how I was raised, and more of the choices I made in heated moments.

In any case, my first fight was in the third grade, and by grade six I was fighting regularly. The projects where we lived were filled with Black families. Those were the kids I started fighting with first, and later I took on the Puerto Ricans as well. Being the only Cuban, I felt I had a culture and heritage to uphold, and I didn't take shit from anyone. My Cuban pride made me fearless.

What all those fights did, as destiny would have it, was prepare me for the next stage in my evolution. It's like I was silently, invisibly, being guided in a direction, a kind of apprenticeship or initiation into the criminal life. The first stage transitioned to stage two. Bit by bit the stakes would be raised, and every step of the way I took the bait.

I was around twelve years old when I was first approached to burn down a car. The task was simple enough: throw a brick through the window, and torch the vehicle from the inside. It paid $200. At this time burning down cars and businesses was gaining in popularity as a means to collect insurance money. From this insurance scam, the term "burn down era" was coined.

My friends and I took to this scam hard and fast. We were gaining a reputation. The strange thing was, I wasn't doing it for the money. Unlike my friends, my parents had decent jobs and I wasn't lacking for any of the essentials. For me, it was about being part of something, part of a group. It was exciting. Eventually I got on the radar of a truancy officer because I was out causing chaos instead of being at school. I knew Officer Vicks because he patrolled our neighborhood and one day, he nailed me for stealing a car. When you're that age they hold you until your parents fetch you from the station, which my mom did. But I was right back on the streets after that, getting even bolder in my twisted trade. We stole cars like it was nothing. All I needed was a screwdriver and, in a few seconds, I would break in, jam the screwdriver into the ignition, turn it on and drive away. I even started showing up to school in these stolen cars, which was definitely a stupid idea because soon enough I was arrested again. Maybe that was the point. Maybe in my own adolescent mind, I was showing everybody how far I was willing to go, how much I didn't care what the consequences were. And there definitely would be consequences. Year by year, they would get more severe, until, as you've already read, I would be stuffed into a concrete cell no bigger than the average bathroom to face the legacy of my choices. But as a kid I couldn't see that yet, or I just didn't care. My parents did care, though. In fact, they had had enough of my antics and had arranged a change of atmosphere, a radical change. They announced that I would be sent to Las Vegas, where my aunt, my father's sister lived, along with four of my father's adult sons from previous marriages. I went, and I was not happy about the arrangement.

My aunt Hilda met me at the Vegas airport, along with two of my half-brothers. It was the first time I had met this side of the family, all of whom had come over from Cuba in 1980 during the El Mariel exodus, when Fidel Castro made a deal with the US government that anyone who wanted to leave Cuba could do so. Many of these Cubans arrived in Florida on crowded boats, including my aunt and step-brothers.

I was immediately impressed with my new environment. Aunt Hilda lived in a nice condo building with big glass windows, the kind of luxury I was not used to coming from the projects in the Bronx. I had my own bedroom. The plan was to stay in Vegas indefinitely, using the summer break to look for a school to enroll in for the fall. My aunt took the initiative to find me a school and I went with her to visit a couple of them. Meanwhile I was spending more time with my adult half-brothers, especially Federico. The two of us hit it off. Soon enough, I was spending more time at his place than at my aunt's. It came to a point that I wasn't even going to my aunt's anymore. He even took me out on a camping trip with his girlfriend and his girlfriend's daughter, who was my age. Out there on a lake by the mountains, it felt good. I was a long way from the concrete jungle of my hood.

Federico also had a motor scooter, which he would let me take out and ride around the city. He padded my pockets with some spending money, a hundred bucks here, another hundred there. And let's not forget about his girlfriend's daughter, the one I started fooling around with. There was a kid our age who lived in my brother's neighborhood, a white guy named Steve, and he became a part of our small crew. We would go out on the town, drink beers and stroll through the casinos on The Strip, coming home at one or two in the morning. All in all, Vegas was turning into one big vacation.

While living with Fede my other brother Jose would come over, and I noticed that there would always be a lot of private conversations in Spanish between them and packages changing hands. That's when I started to have my suspicions. One night I was left alone, and decided to do some investigating. There was a bedroom on one side of the apartment that I was told was private, a room for the "saints" that I was not to enter. As a teenage boy this of course made me more than curious, so I crept over to the door and opened it as soon as I was alone.

The first thing I noticed were the icons of the Catholic saints on the walls of the dark room, giving it an atmosphere of peace and serenity. There was Santa Barbara with her crown and red dress, San Lazaro dressed in rags with his dog and cane, and La Virgen de la Caridad holding baby Jesus, two angels on each side of her.

But as my eyes scanned the rest of the room, I spotted some neatly stacked packages in the corner. My suspicions were confirmed: cocaine and marijuana, and lots of it. What's more, there was a white lump of coke on a plate by the packages. Inspired by what I had seen in Scarface I rushed in and started pulling it into my nostrils. When I added some booze and weed to the mix, things went sideways. I was getting high, very high. In fact, in my haste to consume everything I could at the same time, I got so high that I blacked out. It was Fede who woke me up hours later. He was upset, but not angry. From then on, my brothers didn't hide their business from me, moving product right in front of my face.

What I soon learned was that this was no small-time operation. Not only were all of my four half-brothers involved, but it turned out that my aunt was their ringleader. That's right, she was the head of a major drug dealing operation. Now it all made sense—her fancy clothes, the luxury condo, her Cadillac and the driver that took her everywhere.

Eventually word got around to my parents that I was no longer staying at Hilda's place, so they sent my sister Glenda to scope out the situation. They were already weary because of Federico's history; he spent a few years in prison in Cuba before coming to the US. In fact, it was a point of pride for Fidel Castro that he had sent many criminals to the US as part of the El Murial agreement, as he was more than happy to hand the burden over to his enemy, the US government.

Glenda came to Vegas with her son, my nephew, and her boyfriend. She took to the Vegas life right away and ended up marrying her boyfriend and staying.

Still, my parents were never going to leave me in Vegas with this crew, so they got on a plane, stayed for a week, and dragged me back to the hood with them. Which meant my Vegas party had sadly come to a close.

NEW YORK
GIANTS
ny

CHAPTER FOUR

WHEN I GOT back, Vegas was inside of me, you couldn't remove what I had seen and experienced. The money, the glamor, the lifestyle, it all rubbed off. When I returned to New York I hit the ground running with dreams of being the next Pablo Escobar– and I was only thirteen years old! This was right in the middle of New York's crack epidemic. Heroine was also rampant. A couple of guys in our crew started experimenting, but I wanted no part of the crack pipe. That was for good reason because when P.J. and Hector began smoking that stuff, they were gone. They disappeared in more ways than one. Crack was no joke and ended up annihilating too many young lives.

Because of these drugs, people were making money. There were teenagers in the hood getting rich. We saw it. Fifteen- and sixteen-year-olds pulling up in Lambos and Caddis. Some had the retractable license plates you saw in James Bond movies. Till this day, when I think of my past, it all seems like a film. Back then we used the term "making a movie" often to describe our scene and what we did.

Manuel, basically my best friend out of the crew, made the first connection that got us into the crack and heroin trade. He found a girl who was willing to front us the product. Our take was 30 percent of every hundred sold. We started with five thousand worth, and the stuff moved fast. Two days tops. We split the profit four ways, about $800 a piece, not bad for a couple days' work. Truth be told, it didn't even take much effort. All we did was hang on our corner drinking and smoking weed, while the customers came to us. Then we would take the train into the city to go and splurge on clothes, jewelry, or go to the movies.

It was during one of those trips into Manhattan that we were christened with our name. About ten of us were on the train when we ran into a few dudes from an organization called the 5 Percenters. They were a big network made up of mostly Black guys that had created a mythology around their existence. Having dropped their given names, they took on handles with a mythic quality like Justice, Sincere and Infinity. In other words, they liked names with symbolic meanings that were easy to understand. Seeing that our crew was almost entirely Puerto Ricans, this big dude got all excited and used the P and the R, and said, "Yo, you're The Power Rules." From that day forward that's who we told the world we were, and it accelerated our mission of mayhem even more.

The business grew. We expanded to other corners, built a reputation. Manuel made other connections, got us more weight to move. We were having fun and making money. The product didn't need much promotion other than passing out some free samples and telling people to spread the word. After that, the users and addicts would flow to us like water from a fountain. It was easy money. Along with moving our product on the street, I was still stealing cars when the opportunity arose and robbing other dealers. By this time, I had been booked a few times, and finally they arrested me on multiple stolen car charges. This resulted in a ten-month sentence at Spofford, a juvenile detention facility. I spent the first few months of my sentence there, then I was moved to a group home in Far Rockaway, Queens. During my ten months stay I was still allowed to go home on weekends and on holidays. You'd think that by now, I'd start correcting my ways, but the opposite was true. On one of those mini trips back to my hood I was with my crew from The Power Rules, doing what we did, general mischief, and I caught another case. My parents paid the $500 bail, and the charges were eventually dropped. I finished my time in the group home and was right back on the streets.

By now you may be asking yourself, where were his parents? Believe me, they kept trying to help bring me around. My mother used to beg me to stop my delinquent ways. She told me they would buy me whatever I needed, clothes, a car, as long as I quit the streets and went to school. For some reason, none of it got through. I nodded, told my parents what they wanted to hear, and got right back in the game.

Upon my return from Spofford and the group home, not only had Manuel grown the business, but it seemed like everyone in the streets was selling something. Which meant more heat. The police presence was constant. They would come around and sweep the hood on a regular basis, but we simply didn't care. We went from clearing a couple hundred dollars a day, to a grand a day, each. Manuel bought a newer Boneville, I bought a Honda. It wasn't only our car situation which was improving, it was our firepower too. From six shot revolvers we graduated to military grade weapons—we're talking M-16s, Uzis, Tec 9s. I bought my own MAC-10, a compact machine gun. We learned to use them on the roof of our building, up on the twenty-first floor. That's right, you're reading that correctly. We were doing live fire drills in the middle of a busy city, into the open sky. The Bronx was like its own third world country, our own Beirut and that's what we would call it sometimes.

One day while we were working one of our spots on Union Ave., the cops showed up. But this wasn't just any typical visit, a cruiser scoping out the scene. They pulled up in a van, and a full on Tactical Narc Team (TNT) emptied out of it. As their name suggests, the TNT were a group of counter narcotics agents created in the aftermath of a slain police officer at the hand of a drug dealer. Even up against this elite, well trained and armed unit, we weren't going down easily. I was with my friends Titus and Tommy and we bolted into the building. They chased after us. We got to the stairs and Titus used the opportunity to flash his loaded Uzi, which made the TNT cops panic and scatter, slowing them down.

We got to the roof, the TNT right on our heels. They tackled Tommy while Titus and I launched ourselves from rooftop to rooftop.... just like in the movies.

Somehow our making movie motto became an actuality in our real lives. We ended up on the roof of our friend Victor's building, and took the stairwell down to his apartment. He was there with his mother. We paid him some money and celebrated our brazen escape from the law. Maybe we did a bit too much celebrating because a few minutes later the festivities were interrupted by a loud bang and crash—a battering ram. The TNT broke down Victor's door and were using the captured Tommy as a body shield in case we opened fire. Tommy's face was a mess. The cops had given him a straight up beat down. They threw Victor to the ground along with his mother, who had nothing to do with our scene. Then it was my turn. They threw me on the floor and I felt a boot come down on my neck. "Not so tough now, are you?" the cop yelled, making sure my face got a good chafing as he applied more pressure to the backside of my head and neck. I'm sure he got some pleasure from the choking sounds I made as I struggled for air. Then they clamped the handcuffs onto my wrists, making sure to tighten them to the point where pain shot up my arm. I was yanked to my feet from behind, again orchestrated for maximum pain, and taken to the waiting van. The three of us were thrown inside. I couldn't believe it, but they had caught others as well, unrelated to our take down. I knew one guy, Pete, from the hood.

"They got you too," he said with a smile on his face.

Our first stop was central booking on 161st St. We were placed in a large cage called a bullpen with ten to fifteen other men awaiting a hearing with a judge. At that time, it took up to four days to get to your first hearing, meanwhile you were stuck in this cage like animals, with only one toilet out in the open. To put it bluntly you had to piss and shit in front of people, a process as degrading and dehumanizing as it sounds. It was because of those conditions and wait times that things changed in 1992, and it was mandated that you had to see a judge within twenty-four hours of your arrest. A bit too late for us since the events I'm describing here occurred in late '89.

The judge set my bail at $1500 and I was sent to Riker's Island for the first time. I arrived at the infamous C-74 unit, which was also known as C-74, Adolescents At War.

Straight off the bat the place lived up to its name. You were admitted with your street clothes, and because of my success on the streets, I had some very desirable things on me. Particularly the chains on my neck, the boots on my feet, and the hoodie on my back.

As I was escorted to my unit, I immediately drew the attention of the other young inmates. I could hear their voices coming through the doors of each holding room as I passed them in the hallway, their faces pressed up against the glass: "Yo, those boots are mine... Naw man, I saw 'em first... I'll take them jeans... then I got the chain."

The guard opened a door and I was brought into an open room with about fifty young men my age, between the ages of sixteen and eighteen. I was led to my cot, which was beside other cots that lined the walls and filled the middle of the room. The guard left me there, like a sheep surrounded by wolves. But I was not a sheep and the others were about to find that out. It was only a few minutes before the first guy came up on me, a Spanish guy of all people, one of my own.

"Nice boots," he said. "They be people in here that want them."

Here's what I always knew– to have fear inside of you is normal, but on the streets and in jail, you can't let anyone get even a hint of it. Because once they do, it's like a predator on its prey. Don't let anyone have an inch.

"You see these boots? Come on, take a good look," I said. "They're staying right where they are, on my feet."

He lets out a sigh. This tells me he is thinking fast, assessing the situation and his chances.

"You sure about that?"

I remain stone faced.

Then it comes. In the kind of life I lived, you went from throwing words to fists in a half second. He went in first and I came right back at him. The COs were sent it and broke it up. As I told the kid, the boots would stay on my feet. I was willing to take on the whole place if I had to.

That same day, contestant number two stepped up to test his luck. I wasn't sure who else might jump in so my nerves were frayed. Still, I fought him as well and kept what was mine. Then the night came and my anxiety grew. Once I was asleep anyone could come over and just yank the boots off my feet. As for taking them off, there was no way I was doing that. So I ended up lying awake in my bed all night, ready to fend off any and all attacks, with my boots laced up tight.

One thing you should know is when you're in and out of Juvi and prisons like we all were, there's always people you know on the inside. The next day at mess hall I ran into one of those acquaintances, a kid named Fred. Word about me had already gotten around.

"Dudes be scheming on you homie," he said. "I'll put in a word to my man Born." Born was a 5 Percenter, the group I mentioned earlier, and it looked like he had some pull in my dorm. Fred was able to get a guarantee from Born, it wasn't ideal but it was something. I would not be jumped by a gang, but I was fair game for anyone that wanted to take me on, one on one.

I had a few more fights before I got word that my parents had bailed me out. I left C-74 with my head high and, as I vowed, the boots on my feet and the clothes on my back.

D SITTING
E EATING
F PICTURES
A FUMAR
B ABRAZARSE
C BESOS
D SENTARSE

CHAPTER FIVE

ONCE I WAS back at my parents place, I did a rare thing; I laid low. I was beat up and dirty. I threw away the clothes I had on for those few days, I hadn't changed out of them since I was booked. Everything about where I was held in central booking and Riker's disgusted me. I didn't want the residue of that stench anywhere on my body.

By now, my parents truly feared for me. "You're going to get killed in the street my boy. You're still so young," they told me in Spanish. Those weren't just words.

There were parents in the hood who came knocking on apartment doors now and then, raising money because they couldn't afford to bury their slain kids. That must have really had an impact on my father, because he went out and bought life insurance as well as burial plots for us all. If something happened, he wanted to be prepared. No one from our family would be knocking on doors to beg for money if my father had anything to do about it.

A couple of rest days and I hit the streets again. Now the TNT had sights on us. They were getting a better hold of the drug scene, which meant the business changed. We were still selling but not to the same degree. Old timers from the hood were filtering back, having served their sentences. They were older than us, and thought they could come back and pick up where they left off by working their old corners. We made it clear that the turf was now ours. If they wanted to work, they would have to go through us. We may have been young, but we were loaded down with arms, and ruled like warlords. So, the old timers got in line, but instead of moving product and taking a percentage of the proceeds, they started sticking up other dealers and stealing their product outright to resell. That way it would be a 100 percent profit rather than 30 or 40 percent. And while they were at it, if the dealer had any jewelry, they would take that as well. Some of our guys had so much stolen metal around their neck and on wrists and fingers, they looked like Mr. T. It was ridiculous.

I started to look the part as well, but Gretel, my sister who I was closest to in age, five years older than me, was not impressed.

"Don't think you look cute," she said to me. "You don't even look Cuban anymore." My oldest sister Glenda felt the same way. In their own way everyone in the family was doing what they could to get through my very thick head. Little did they know, it would take a lot more than words to turn me around. As far as I was concerned, it was all or nothing—I dove into the action, with few barriers or brakes. It was all about movement, action, excitement. Making movies as we called it.

That's how we ended up jumping into a car, eight of us this time. We were after a rival gang member because of some dispute over a girl, the details of which aren't clear to me now and were never that important at the time. We heard the kid was hanging out by Gompers High School, so we drove up and spotted him. All eight of us emptied out the car, started beating on the kid and jumped him. At some point another car showed up and we heard gunshots. We scattered. I was running away from the scene toward Union Ave., when I felt my left side getting heavier. "Yo, you bleeding," someone called out.

I stopped and assessed the situation. There was blood on my shirt, on the lower left side. Without calling the cops or an ambulance, my friends took me to the hospital, where I was seen by the doctors and X-rays were taken—a flesh wound to the back. The bullet was lodged in there. I was given a choice: leave it in, or have it removed, though with the removal option was a risk since the bullet was embedded close to my spine.

Of course, my parents were distraught. I had caused them further pain, once again, in this seemingly never-ending cycle of youthful madness. The movie continued.

I was told our crew regrouped and retaliated a few hours later. Apparently, a couple of the guys they shot up were in the very same hospital, down in the ER.

That night my mother spent the night with me in the hospital room, sleeping on a cot beside my bed. No matter what I did, my mother was always by my side.

No surprise, once I was healed up, I was back in the mix and taking pleasure in my new obsession, sticking up drug dealers. I got a rush out of it, I was always on the hunt for the next take down. Unlike me, my best friend in our crew, Manuel, was not happy with the stick-up scene. He told me so one night while we were on the block doing the usual, hanging out and smoking blunts. Pete and Jose showed up, telling us they saw a guy on Southern Boulevard who owed them money.

That's all I needed to hear to get all hyped, like a soldier called up for duty. But Manuel had his own ideas.

He pulled me aside for a talk: "Don't go... this is small time shit."

"You're like my parents. You worry too much," I said to him.

"I'm telling you, it's not worth it."

"I'll be back in no time."

"You know I'm just looking out for you."

"Ya, course."

"We're brothers," he said.

"I know that."

We took each other's hand, brought it in for an embrace. That was the thing with me and Manuel, no matter what happened, what disagreements we had, nothing got in the way of our friendship. We were bonded like blood brothers.

So I went with Pete and Jose. Pete spotted the guy and we made our move, descending on him with fists and arms. We beat him enough to send the message that Pete wrapped up with the final words: "Get me my money, or next time we kill you." The kid got up and bolted. Mission accomplished.

Just like I told Manuel, we came back to our corner. No worries. That was until the cops pulled up and arrested us, and it was the whole process all over again. First to 161st St., then into the cage to await my hearing.

"See, I told you," Manuel said to me at one point when I spoke to him on the phone. "I felt it, I knew you shouldn't have gone."

You see, I wouldn't even listen to my best friend's advice.

This time I got nailed for armed robbery, even though we weren't armed. The kid we jumped either lied, or was put up to it so we would get a stiffer sentence.

The judge set the bail at $3500, a sum my parents couldn't pay. I was taken to Riker's Island for my second stay.

On this occasion I had the latest sneakers on and had to fight to keep those on my feet. That is until I heard the loudspeaker in the dorm call out my name:

"William Licea, report to the bubble. William Licea, report to the bubble."

I went to see the CO. He told me to collect my things.

"Where am I going?"

"Don't you want to get out of here?"

I hurried to grab my possessions and followed him out of the dorm. Apparently, the angels were still with me. Manuel had come through and paid my bail after only a couple days at Riker's.

The voices, more voices, all those voices who were on the side of reason and sanity tried to break through to me.

My girlfriend: "You need to stop this."

Her parents: "We hear what you guys are doing in the streets…. time to make better choices. Before it's too late."

My mother: "Mi hijo, precioso… todavia eres tan joven."

I was appointed a public defender. He was pushing me to take a plea deal, as opposed to going to trial. Which meant a one and a half to four-and-a-half-year sentence, as opposed to a much longer one if I went to trial and lost. He told me not to play with the taxpayer's money, to strike a deal. I think what he most wanted was to get my case over with and move on. I took his advice and plead guilty and was told to report back in sixty days for my prison sentence.

By now, maybe you can guess what I did. That's right, I didn't report back. I jumped bail, testing my limits and fate for the dozenth time. But in my trade, as the stakes got higher, as I got older, my so-called days of freedom became shorter and shorter. Eventually, the inevitable always does come around. The screws tighten. The hunter becomes the hunted.

A couple of months later, at 5am one morning while I slept in my bedroom, in my parents house, my girlfriend Aracelis beside me, the warrant squad came knocking. My father opened the door.

"Is William here?"

My father shrugged.

"I don't know where he is," he said.

They shoved him aside, pushed their way in, picked me up off of my comfortable bed, and took me into captivity.

There's a lot of noise about what happens in prison and some of it is true. You've probably heard about overcrowding, the terrible conditions, fighting, riots, weapons, drugs and violence—I've experienced it all. But no one seems to talk about the toilets at Riker's. As in what they're used for apart from the obvious.

When you're thrown in there with the clothes on your back, it begs the question what do you do when your jeans get dirty? After all, prison is not a hotel. When I was there in the '90, no one came around to do your laundry, so you were forced to get creative. That's where the toilet bowl came in—it doubled as a wash basin. You dipped your jeans in and got to work, scrubbing, rinsing, then hanging them up to dry.

The toilets were also your fridge on hot days. The commissary sold cold cuts, so to keep them cold you sealed up the bag and put them in the toilet water. We did that with water bottles as well, unbelievable as that sounds.

Since the beginning of time humans have found ways to adapt and survive in different conditions, often hostile ones. Prison was no exception. This time I would need to find a way to do both—adapt and survive—because once I was taken in after jumping bail, I had a year and a half bid to get through.

I started at Riker's, was sent to Ulster County for a month, and finally settled in Georgetown for the majority of my sentence. Georgetown was a minimum-security camp, which meant it was more relaxed and easy going than your medium or max security prison.

The one thing they did there was put you to work. I cut down trees for firewood every morning and cleaned trash off the side of the highway.

You could even make fires and cook your own food outside. My parents and girlfriend came to visit every couple of weeks. There was very little violence apart from the odd shoving match. All in all, it was the best prison could be.

Even with better conditions in this prison, there was something in me at that time, at that age, call it a mania, that seemed destined to turn a good thing sour. I was sitting on a park bench with my girlfriend Aracelis on one of her visits when I got to touching her. It was a bit too much for the CO, so he called me over.

"You've been told the rules. One kiss when she comes in, one when she leaves."

"Come on, man. Just look the other way."

"It doesn't work like that here."

"What, you mad cause your girl don't look like this?"

I was getting in his face, instead of backing off and heeding his words.

"Listen, I said keep your hands to yourself."

That's all it took. The CO wrote me a ticket and said I threatened him. I was put in solitary and then moved to another prison, one in which I didn't have nearly the freedoms and privileges I had at Georgetown.

I finished out my sentence at Gouvernor, a medium security state prison and was given back my freedom after a year-and-a-half, my longest stint up until that point. The year was 1992. I was still only eighteen.

One month. That's the amount of time my freedom lasted. One month before me, Julian and Pedro jammed our guns into the face of that dealer by Longwood Ave., took his cash and jewelry, and got arrested not even a half hour later.

That was the moment that I not only stole from someone, but would lead to another kind of theft. That of my youth and the prime years of my life– time that was taken from me and I'll never get back.

It was the moment that it all caught up with me. I've heard it said that when a criminal does wrong, in their subconscious mind what they really want is to get caught. Police are baffled sometimes by the obvious clues that are left at a crime scene, as if on purpose. As a kid in the streets I can tell you deeper motivations were not on my mind. But if you look at what I was doing, day in and day out, I was daring the gods and society to hear me, to see me, to deal with me. I would dare them over and over and over again, at each turn popping up with an act more brazen and outrageous.

It was all inside of me, this inner drive, which kept pushing me, its motives unknown, a mystery.

I dared, pushing things as far as I could take them, until the inevitable. Society finally paid attention and acknowledged me for what I was. I was lucky I didn't lose my life. Is this what I was really after all along?

It would be two decades before I would be a free man again.

NEW YORK
KNICKS

CHAPTER SIX

IT'S 1997. I'M in Sing Sing, that notorious prison north of the city, sitting in the box—again—four-and-a-half years into my original nine-year bid.

The box, solitary, is just you and the four concrete walls. I guess prison wasn't enough for me, I needed a prison inside a prison, and that second prison became the container for my mind.

Here there was no escaping yourself. It made me face my situation, what I was up against. Time is a hell of a thing. Everything in prison is about time. It's a clock, forever counting down to the end of your bid. And then there's the time you're given in the box, your shorter sentence within a longer one.

Prison is about time, and the box gives you plenty of it. A saying comes to me, which I would repeat in prison, over and over through those days, months and years.

"As long as the sun doesn't burn out, as long as the water doesn't run dry and I keep myself sane, this too shall pass."

Keeping sane was one of the keys, because people do lose their minds in solitary. We're built for human interaction, and when you don't get it, you can go to a dark place. That's why I always knew the ultimate battle was to stay sane. In the box it's 23-1—as in twenty-three hours inside those four solitary walls, and one meager hour outside. One hour in the yard to make up for the other twenty-three, rain, sleet, or snow. The weather gives the COs another excuse to mess with you. If it's cold out, they'll give you your hour, and if they feel particularly sadistic, may leave you out for an extra thirty minutes. When it comes time to let you out the next day, they'll use the previous day's experience as leverage to ask: "You sure you want your hour today? It's cold out there..." And when the weather was nice and warm and sunny, you'd get the opposite, COs finding any excuse to pull you in early. Let's just say that when people have this kind of power over you, they can play some weird games. I'm sure in their position, dealing with the hardened criminals that we were, it was easy to justify their behavior in their own minds, and it does add to your own burden of thinking that you're no better than an animal, an insect even. This treatment begs the question: Is the time you serve in prison enough of a price to pay for what you've done, or should you also be put in situations where you're demeaned and mistreated, in subtle and not so subtle ways? Going a bit deeper the question may be, are you still human? Taking into account some of my worst experiences in the system, the answer would have to be no.

Twenty-three, one. Hours split apart and broken up. It's all a game with time, minutes inside hours, cells inside rooms and boxes inside cells. For the first time I read books. I got into David Morrell—First Blood, The Brotherhood of the Rose, Fraternity of The Stone.

I was lonely and these books kept me company. Their words penetrated into my stubborn mind. They showed me it was possible to survive under almost any condition as long as you didn't give up. They also taught me about principles and morals, things I hadn't really let myself ponder up to then. There were other lessons in those books too– how to handle a knife, deflect punches, knock someone out with the palm of your hand. Believe it or not, I practiced those self-defense skills in the box and later with other inmates, and the techniques worked. They would save me more than once. It was as if God put those books in my cell just at the right moment, when I needed them the most.

I was being prepared. There was something just over the horizon that had been with me since 1990, and it was during that stint in the box that it became real. Again, it was time doing its thing, playing its tricks, the past waiting there to be reeled into the present.

One afternoon a CO came to my cell to tell me I had visitors. I was taken out of the cell and led to a private meeting room. There, I was briefed by another of the warden's men that I had two visitors from the Feds, and asked if I was willing to speak to them. Curious as to what they wanted, I said yes.

The two men were waiting inside a private room on one side of a metal table. One guy, thin and blonde with a mustache introduced himself as agent Rick, the other guy with black hair was from the FBI. Both wore dress shirts and slacks. Once I was seated on the other end of the table, the DEA guy started in:

"How're you doing, Will?"

"Fine, you know, all considered."

"Everything good with you?"

"As good as it can be in here," I said, keeping it light.

The small talk went back and forth for a bit. I noticed the FBI guy with the black hair was mostly observing.

"We heard a lot about you actually. People on the street talk, you know."

Yeah, sure, I knew. I definitely knew he was getting to something important in the next few seconds.

"We know about The Power Rules," he continued. I didn't even nod, just stayed as stoned faced as possible. The FBI guy did the same, keeping his stone face, looking at me, hands folded in front of him on the table.

"We also know you were a lieutenant with The Power Rules, the right-hand man of your associate, Manuel."

No one had ranks in our group, so the lieutenant thing was funny and totally off base.

"And you know what else we know Will...? October 14th., 1990. Ring a bell?"

"No."

"That's strange because your friend Antonio lost his life that day. And people are saying you're the one who did it."

As I said the following words—"I have no idea what you're talking about"—my insides were in free fall. I was suddenly dizzy and doing my best to hide my interior turmoil.

Agent Rick leaned closer to me now. He said, "The Power Rules are sinking and we're sending you a life line. All you need to do is take it."

He got the part about sinking right. I was sinking, on the verge of drowning.

"If not, in two weeks you'll be indicted for racketeering and the murder of Antonio Juan Morales. You'll be facing a life sentence." Thinking back on it now, the FBI agent must have seen a change in my demeanor. After seven years, the past not only haunted me, but was back in my face, and wanted retribution.

"I never murdered anyone," I said.

"You're going to sink Will, with all your friends. Unless... I'm sure you know how this goes."

"I had nothing to do with this, so..."

"One last time. We're your life boat. How do you want this to end? It can't be with you dying of old age in a prison cell."

I had nothing left to say. No matter what, I was not about to cooperate. Even if the consequences were dire. I stayed quiet until they announced that the meeting was over and stepped out of the room.

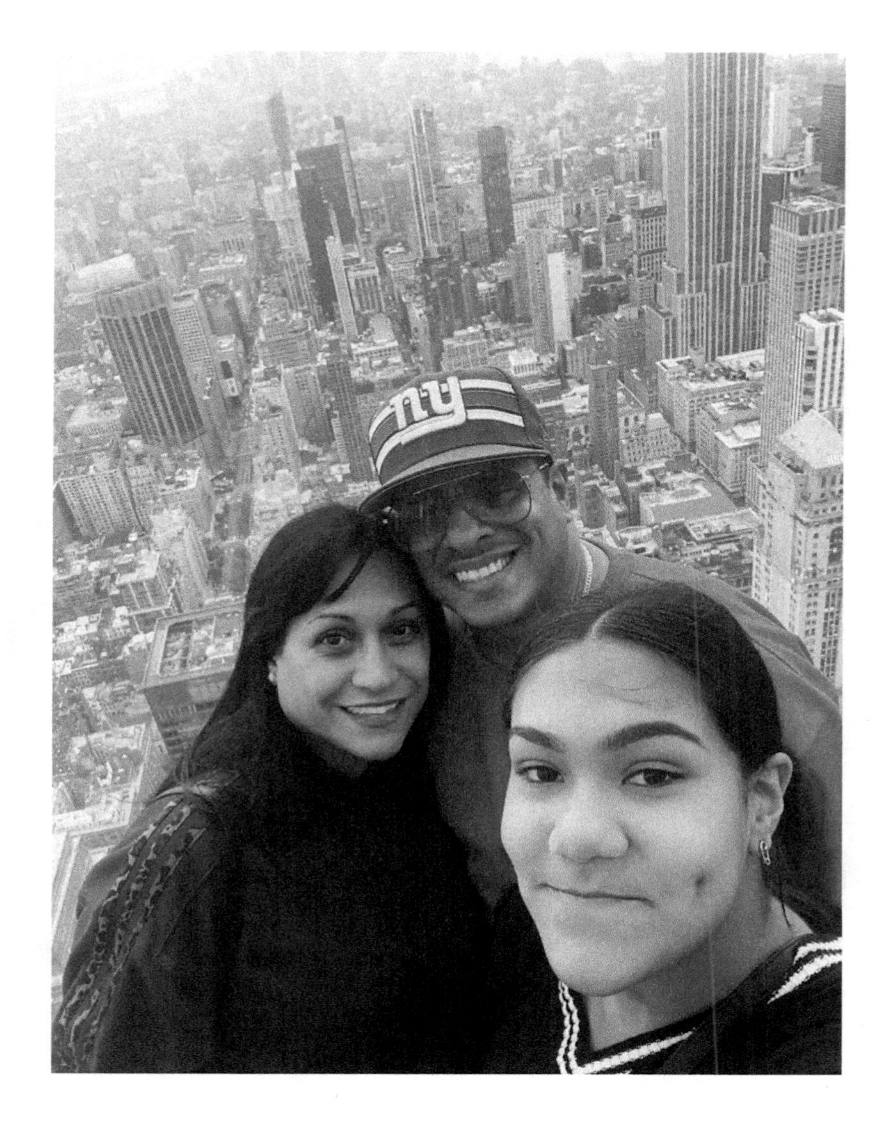
ny

SIGNAGE
SIGNAGE

CHAPTER SEVEN

THAT DAY IN October of 1990 will never leave me, no matter where I go or how much I change.

I was sixteen. We, The Power Rules, had this ongoing war with the Dominicans. With as much money circulating in the street those days, it was to be expected that we'd have some competition. But that didn't mean we liked or tolerated it. Our crew would roll up in the cold light of day, pull out our military hardware, and rob rival gangs right out in the open. As if that wasn't humiliating enough, we'd celebrate our triumphs in front of them. Any chance we could get, we would show the neighborhood who was in control. But you can't do that repeatedly and not expect some retaliation.

In the street life there's always some beef, some drama that someone's dealing with. Word of these disputes travels fast and was often the motivation for a lot of our activity. It didn't even matter what the beef was, as long as there was one.

That's how I found myself driving my man Edgar's Camaro IROC-Z into Dominican territory. One of our guys had a beef with one of theirs. I wasn't even sure what it was and didn't care. The only thing that mattered was that we were moving with speed and purpose.

We spotted them on the block, milling around outside a building, and pulled over. As soon as they saw us exit the car, they came running toward us with their guns ablaze. We dove back in the car hearing the dull thud of metal piercing metal, and peeled out of there. The amazing thing was no one was hit.

We retreated back to our block and planned a counter attack. This was war and of course I wanted to lead the charge.

With that same pock marked IROC-Z, we headed back into battle. This time we were better prepared. There was PK, loaded up with an M-16, a couple others with Uzis and me, with my MAC 10. Like I said, military grade hardware.

I jump out the driver's side, PK out the passenger door. When my feet hit the ground I was spraying bullets. I recognize one of their guys, I even remember his name, Ricky, who let loose earlier on our car, and I emptied my clip in his direction. From that moment my memory is a blur. I saw people drop but couldn't be sure if they were hit or just got low to duck the incoming fire.

We hit and ran, back to home base, and put the guns away. Then we decided to take the train into the city. We wound up in Central Park, enjoying the day, carrying on like nothing had happened. When we return to the Bronx, there's big news. It was a fog of war moment and it went like this– as I came out of the car and opened fire on their guy Ricky, one of our guys, Antonio, who lived in the building with the Dominicas, happened to be coming out the door. Ricky threw him in front to protect himself. Antonio was hit and killed. By mistake.

His death made the news that night. I was distraught. PK got arrested. I was afraid he would be pressured into snitching, but he ended up following the code of the streets and kept his mouth shut. Eventually PK had the case dismissed due to a lack of evidence. That's the last we heard of it. Even though it seemed that we were home free, Antonio's death stayed with me, as if waiting for the reality of it to reappear at any moment. Which it did.

Just as the federal agents from the FBI and DEA had warned me, I was indicted for murder two weeks after their visit. Yes, that final domino of my life on the streets fell. Someone had broken the street code and spoke to the Feds. I was appointed a public defender once again and offered a thirty year sentence instead of life if I copped a plea. I told my lawyer I would rather try my luck and go to trial. After a year and a half of back and forth dealings, they offered twenty years running concurrent with my sentence and I agreed, which meant I now had eleven and a half years to serve in total. The last decade of which would be in Federal custody.

Even though I was a prison veteran by this point, I was still only twenty-six years old, barely an adult. Once again, the question of time. How to make sense of the decade plus in front of me and that behind me, what I had done, and what I had seen? Prison, what a dog from hell. Shit, piss, violence and death, that's what happens inside those four walls, and they move in on you little by little.

At first, it's invisible. You can't see them, but they're there, just past your sightline. The streets trick you into a certain kind of wild belief, one you may not even acknowledge to yourself. You begin to believe that the days will pass, and there won't be a price to pay.

Almost as certain as death, those walls will appear, even though you won't know the hour. And then what? It's as bad inside as it is on the exterior. Some fool dies in front of you over a gold chain in his last week of prison because his pride won't allow him to give it up. So, he gets a knife in the chest, and passes his last moments, sliding down one of those concrete walls as he takes his last breath. The absolute absurdity of it, senseless, and idiotic. To die for a damn chain.

Would that be me, dying a pathetic death? Truth is, it could be any of us, the dogs of hell could take you at any moment.

So, you play your role, and do your best to stay alive. Sure, life on the outside is about survival, but survival is more apparent and urgent on the inside. By now my girlfriend Aracelis has moved on. Two decades is a long stretch to wait for someone. Yes, time plays with us all.

It's 1999, I've been moved from one prison to the next and end up at the Upstate Correctional, a straight SHU facility. Meaning inmates from all over New York are sent here to do time in solitary. In my case it's eight months for taking part in a prison chapel riot. I guess you could say we had a knack for turning the sacred into the profane.

In all the time I had spent in solitary, it was just me and the four walls, until Upstate where everyone got a roommate. With so many people flowing into the prison system they were starting to economize.

Unlike normal prison conditions, here you got no phone calls. Your only contact with the outside world was through written correspondence, letters. And the less you heard, the more you worried about.

One morning in early August the CO came into my cell and told me to get dressed. "The chaplain wants to see you," he said. I threw on a shirt, my hands got cuffed and I was escorted to the chaplain's office.

Once I was there, the mood was already somber.

"Why don't you have a seat, William."

In his mid-forties, the chaplain was soft spoken, reserved. Much different than the kind of people I was used to hanging around with.

I settled in, on edge. He slipped off my handcuffs. I already knew whatever he was about to tell me wasn't good, no one was called to the chaplain for happy news.

"How are things with you?"

I shrugged—what could a person in my position say?

"You probably want to know why you were called in here..."

I nodded, getting restless.

"Yeah, I do."

Then it dropped: "It's your father, Will."

Somehow, I knew it, before he spoke the words.

"He had a heart attack. He's in the hospital. It doesn't look good."

I took it in, in silence.

"We've arranged a phone call, if you like."

"Yes, I'd like to speak to my mother," I said.

He gestured to the phone.

"You sure you're okay?"

Was I being overly stoic? Not really. I just didn't feel the need to suddenly fall apart in front of this man. On the other hand, when I called my mother, she was obviously distraught. She had been with my father for over forty years. But it wasn't just about her grief. She was worried about me, she thought that I might lose my head.

"Listen to me Mamma," I told her in Spanish. "I've been through a lot in here, and I'll get through this."

She passed the phone to my sisters. The message was similar. They both told me to hold it together, to make sure I kept myself on track rather than extend my sentence by doing something irrational. They didn't really know me anymore, and I found this kind of advice annoying.

When our conversation concluded, the chaplain took the phone back and had a word with my mother. She told him she was concerned about me, and worried that I might do something stupid, hinting at suicide.

The one thing I can say about myself, is I have never had a suicidal bone in my body. To me this idea was absurd, an insult even.

Once the chaplain was off the phone I told him in no uncertain terms, that I wasn't the kind of person who would even think about harming themselves. Not even in my darkest hour. I was mindful that at this point my father was seventy-nine years old. His getting older was always in the back of my mind. I was born the last of his ten children when he was fifty-three, not a young man.

"We could get you to the observation cell just to make sure you're alright," the chaplain said, giving it one last shot.

"Nah, I'm good. Just take me to my cell and let me grieve," I answered. He told me if I ever needed to talk with someone, he would always make himself available.

CHAPTER EIGHT

THERE'S A SPECIAL unit that comes for you when you leave the prison grounds. Since we were regarded as the worst of the worst inmates in the system, the first thing they did before taking you from your cell was make sure you were close to incapacitated physically, hands and feet cuffed.

Malone, New York, home to Upstate Correctional was located close to the Canadian border in the northern part of the state. As we sped by the forest that bordered the highway on the long drive to the city, I thought about the things I was missing, life outside of prison. It dawned on me that I had let my mother down, because I couldn't be with her during such a tough time.

This was the first time I had set eyes on the Bronx in seven years. And the Ortiz Funeral Home was in the heart of it, dead center of my old life, like a bull's eye.

On a diagonal was Gompers High School, where I had been shot. Up the street a block, Union Ave. where I used to hang with my crew, and not far in the other direction, 149th St. and Southern Boulevard, where my friend Antonio's life came to an end from a bullet I shot, intended for another person.

We pulled up in front of the funeral home and I saw my sister's husband standing outside waiting for us. He was in a suit, his sidearm clearly visible, clipped into the holster on his belt.

"Who's the guy?" one of the special unit COs asked me. I explained that he was a New York City cop—nothing to worry about.

I was led out of the van, my whole-body clattering with chains. The prison cops address my brother-in-law.

"You got ID for that gun?"

He flashed them his NYPD badge.

"This is my brother," he said. "You can take the cuffs off. I've got him."

To my surprise the prison cops agreed, and released my hand and feet so I could greet my family with at least a bit of dignity.

The beauty of my family was that no matter what happened between us we always remained tight. Together, in the privacy of the funeral home, we grieved over my father who lay silent and still in the casket.

I was only supposed to be given an hour, but the special unit officers were nice enough to extend it another half an hour. At least it gave me a few more moments to be there for my mother, to help comfort her.

I was driven back upstate and they buried my father the next day. My mother would be alone now and that bothered me, so when I later heard that my sister Glenda and her family would be moving in with her, it gave me some relief. With me having to put in another decade plus, I found ease knowing there would be someone in the family to watch over her.

Skyline
N.E.
R-28

CHAPTER NINE

IF YOU BUILD yourself up into thinking you're some kind of God, life will surely show you otherwise. You see your friends get cut down. Some end up in prison while others are laid to rest in the dirt for good.

Not only your friends, but your rivals too. One by one, we fall in one way or another. One by one, we suffer the consequences of our choices, our actions. Maybe if you hang in there long enough, if you give yourself half a chance, you might come to know that even if you're not as infallible as you once thought, even if you've done terrible things and had terrible things done to you, there's at least a guiding hand pushing you along, watching over your life.

Elmira Correctional Facility. Yes, I was transferred to another prison once again. The year was 2000. One of our guys had a beef in the gym with a member of The Brotherhood, a west coast gang who had grown in stature in New York over the course of my close to decade long imprisonment.

This time it was their guy who got stabbed. We met up in the yard with members of their gang, after the fact. Black guys from The Brotherhood, and asked them what they planned to do. Would they retaliate?

They told us it was all good, a one off, a dispute between two men and nothing more.

As the saying went– "We cool."

If you knew well enough, you'd know the Brotherhood were a devious bunch. It was never really clear where you stood with them. They had a reputation for being dirty and underhanded.

A week or two passed. I was in chow hall finishing up a meal. When I was done I dropped off my plates and headed to the door toward my cell. As soon as I was in the corridor, I felt a knife slash across my neck and upper back.

I jerked around to face my attacker and saw there was not just one but four of them there from the Brotherhood, coming at me with fists and knives. With my heart exploding out my chest and adrenaline flooding every vessel of my body, I fought back. The one thing that was clear is they weren't there for a beating, but to take my life.

Somehow, I held them off but I knew it couldn't last long. They were cutting me all over, on my neck, arms, hands. That's when—again like some damn Hong Kong style kung fu movie—I see one of their guys fly across the room. Out of nowhere, my friend Hector had joined the fight. All six feet, five inches of him. This guy was a giant, a bull, and his presence changed everything. Seeing this human wrecking ball must have caused our attackers to second guess themselves because the fight broke up and we all scattered. Without Hector, it's likely I would have been killed that day.

Back in my cell I was cut up, bleeding badly, but I didn't complain or seek medical attention. Instead, I applied tobacco to the wound on my neck, something I had seen done in the movie, *Predator*. I couldn't believe that it worked. I was able to control the bleeding. Hey, we not only made "movies" but we watched and learned from them as well.

The thing about the Brotherhood was they weren't very liked by the COs either. They were constantly playing dirty, saying one thing and doing another.

The next day I was approached in my cell by a CO. He let me know one of the men who jumped me would soon be let out of his cell because he had a visitor coming, and when he was, I could have at him without consequence.

"Their abusers," he said. "They deserve what's coming."

I prepared myself, got together my two homemade steel knives carved from the metal trays in the mess hall. When the time came, I approached him in the gallery and let loose. But he was prepared as well, he had wrapped his arms and chest with books and magazines to protect himself. But that still couldn't stop me. I must have stabbed him twenty-five times before the COs stepped in to end it. I came out of it dazed. The guy was a good fighter and landed a few clean hits across my face and head numerous times.

In the aftermath, the CO who originally let me out, backed me up. He said the other man brought the knives and was the instigator. As I walked back to my cell I was like a prize fighter having taken down the champion. It was my Rocky moment. The rest of the inmates saw the fight as their cells faced the gallery. Many were cheering along with a few of the COs.

Once more, the Brotherhood claimed they did not want a war, but everyone knew their words meant nothing. From the moment I had my victory parade down the hall and made my way back to my cell, I was sure The Brotherhood was planning their revenge.

These were a really sadistic bunch, they knew how to mess with your head. Over the course of the next few weeks, slips of paper found their way into my cell saying I would be killed. I got mail communicating the same message. Even though they were not military men, The Brotherhood knew all about psy-ops tactics, how to spread terror into the heart of the enemy. And it worked. I was in a constant state of paranoia. I not only knew, but felt that my time on this earth could be coming to a fast close. Everyone knew it. They even offered to move me to PC, protective custody, but I refused. The COs pleaded with me.

"We're trying to help you," one said.

If I got killed, it definitely wouldn't look good for the prison, warden, or the system as a whole, especially since the warning shots had already been fired via the many death threats I received.

But I didn't want their help or any special treatment. I knew if I went into protective custody, I would be a target for whatever time I had left to serve in the system. I preferred to take my chances. Despite my paranoia and fears, I thought if my time was truly up, then it was up. At least I would die with a bit of dignity intact.

Suddenly, a sort of miracle happened that changed everything. Since I had served out my state time, the Feds had come for me. Remember, I still had a decade to serve from my plea deal with the Feds for murder and racketeering. I was now property of the Federal government, a whole new jurisdiction with their own prisons.

I say it's a miracle because of the timing. I was whisked out just in time. Two months later, while I was in a federal holding facility in Brooklyn awaiting yet another transfer, another inmate came to me with news:

"You hear about El Mira? They stabbed up some guy in G block."

That was also my block when I was there.

"How bad is he?" I asked.

"Bad as it gets. Threw him under the bed and left him to die."

As soon as I heard that, I knew that could have been me. I was the target all along, and since I was no longer within easy reach, they took out someone else, another Latino man. That's when I began to believe that there was a guiding hand in my life, a divine intervention. The fact that I had escaped certain death, made me think, for the first time, that there might be a bigger plan for my life, some kind of bigger cause.

It was the early stages of my inner shift. Maybe there was hope for me after all. Maybe I could be more than my history of chaos and violence.

Maybe God had other plans for me.

CHAPTER TEN

THE UNITED STATES Penitentiary at Lewisburg was a federal facility located in central Pennsylvania. It had seen the likes of Whitey Bulger, John Gotti, and Jimmy Hoffa come through its gates. Apart from these well-known inmates, it had a reputation for lawlessness and violence, and was the subject of the Academy Award nominated documentary, Doing Time: Life Inside The House.

Knowing the reputation this facility had, and with a full decade left to serve my federal sentence, when I arrived at Lewisburg I knew I had to keep my persona going– the one I had built over the past decade in the state system. Cuban Will, The Wolf. I knew I couldn't let my guard down or I'd quickly become a sheep, and be eaten by the wolves. Especially since I was in a new jurisdiction. It was like I had to prove myself all over again. Like an actor in a movie, there's that role again. I had to stay in character. Now that I was with the Feds, you could say I had graduated, and earned my master's degree, maybe even my PhD, in the criminal life.

As soon as you enter the federal system, the inmates classify you according to where you're from. In state prison, where many inmates are from the five boroughs in New York, I never presented myself as a New Yorker, but Cuban Will, from the Bronx. That was my identity. It separated me from someone from let's say Queens, or Brooklyn. When I came into the federal prison and was asked where I was from, I gave the same answer I had always given, Cuban Will, from the Bronx. The inmate that greeted me yelled out, "New York, we got someone from New York here."

A guy named Daniel, aka Deep, came to greet me by my cell. Of Puerto Rican descent, he was also from the Bronx. Deep was doing multiple life bids for who knows what kind of crimes, definitely not light ones. Many of the inmates I would meet in the feds were straight up lifers, never to experience the outside world again.

Deep asked for my paperwork. I had it on me and presented it to him. This was the informal drill for every new arrival. Since everyone in the federal system came in with official paperwork, or could have access to it within a couple of weeks, it was a way for other prisoners to learn about your history. They were specifically looking for anyone who cooperated with the US government—in other words, snitches. People who testified against their own in order to get a lighter sentence. It was up to the inmate appointed as a sort of intake officer for their state, in my case New York, to clear the new arrival. The paperwork would clearly show this as it did in my case.

I presented my papers to Deep, the pseudo intake officer, and was cleared to move on

since I had never cooperated with the US government despite their best efforts. If your paperwork happened to reveal the opposite, then you were given an ultimatum; go back to the COs and seek protective custody, or the inmates from your home state would be forced to "take one for the team" and make sure you couldn't leave in one piece. We used to say, if a snitch comes in on their feet, then they need to leave on their back. Hey, no one said that prison would be easy.

Another thing you may not know about the prison system is that you can take up a job and only earn pennies per hour. Some of this work is done for major companies, earning them huge profits while the inmates get close to nothing. It's a form of hidden slavery, and I wanted no part of it. That's why I always refused the jobs, even when they were expected, and did not produce products to be sold on the outside. In Lewisburg I was dolled out time in the box for my refusal of such employment, which, on its own, was not so terrible, since I had done so many stints in solitary by now. What really got me was that they could use each infraction and take it away from your good time, adding time to your overall sentence. Through good behavior you could shorten your sentence by 15 percent, which for me was more than a year. The federal system used this as leverage to elicit not only good behavior but compliance, especially from inmates like me who had shorter sentences. This led to me finally taking a job working in the kitchen. Though that did not end well when I got into it with another Cuban, and hit him across the face with a pizza slice and was sent back to my second home, the box.

A year into the decade that I owed the feds, Willy Falcon came into the picture, the person who would become my first true mentor.

By the time I met Falcon he was already a legendary figure. Also of Cuban origin, twenty years older than me, he was one of America's most renowned cocaine distributors. It was claimed that his organization moved almost a million kilos over the course of fifteen years, making him and the people he worked with, wildly wealthy. "The Muchacos," The Boys, as his organization was called, were rumored to have run Miami, even helped build it. He was indicted and taken into federal custody in the early nineties and would spend close to thirty years in prison. Four of those were in Lewisburg, with me, in the same cell. That's right, Willy Falcon was my roommate for close to half a decade, and I can't overstate the influence he had on my thinking and my life.

I wouldn't blame anyone when hearing this to be skeptical—how could someone like Willy Falcon have a positive impact on anyone? On the surface this attitude is perfectly understandable. First of all, I'm here to remind you that people do change. Change is one of the inevitables in life, and that includes inner change.

When my life crossed paths with Falcon's, he was already in his mid to late forties. He had plenty of life experience to share, and he now approached it from a different perspective. I was still just a naive kid from the Bronx. All I knew was my small neighborhood, and the prison system. My thinking was very limited. In many ways I was a petty criminal who couldn't think beyond the borders of my own hood, which included my mind as well. Falcon changed all of that. I guess he saw in me some untapped potential, and it didn't hurt that we were both of Cuban heritage.

Unlike most people I met in the system and on the streets, Falcon was not a corrupter. He never gave criminal advice and never stopped encouraging me to forget about my old life.

"When you get out, leave the ghetto Will," he told me. "Forget your past and your hood friends. Your life will not improve with them around."

It wasn't just what he told me, it was what he did. As I said, he came from a higher place. He was always promoting peace and harmony, and he understood you got that by feeding people, getting them out of their desperate state. After all, if you look at it with eyes wide open, the chaos in prison—and the streets—came from a desperate place, a place of fear.

Falcon did not hesitate to throw around his money to lessen that desperation. If people needed help, he always came through. He would make phone calls to his family on the outside, and have cash sent to inmates' families in need. He really brought a sense of prosperity to the whole unit. And more to the point, he played no favorites. Whether it was a fellow Latino, a member of the

Brotherhood, or whoever else, he made sure to spread the wealth beyond racial, cultural and ethnic lines. Even when you didn't ask, he offered to step in, as was the case with our family.

When my father passed away, as I wrote in the last chapter, my sister and her family went to live with my mother. I learned that the situation eventually turned sour. As my sister's kids got older, they would come in late, making noise, disturbing my mother. She said it was time for her to move, to get her own place. But she needed funds in order to do that.

I told Falcon that the whole thing was stressing me out, that I hated to see my mother unhappy. Falcon asked what my mother needed to get out of the situation. I explained she was short by about six thousand dollars.

"When's your mother next coming for a visit?" Falcon asked, and since I knew what was coming next, I said, "Whenever you need her to, Willy."

Falcon made the arrangements, and when my mother stepped out of her car in the parking lot of the prison that same week to visit me, she was handed an envelope which she slipped quietly into her purse.

I would later find out that not only had Falcon come through with the six grand, but there was an extra two thousand in the envelope.

With that money my mother was able to move to a new apartment. I couldn't thank him enough.

"Will," he told me, "don't worry about it. It's pennies. It's my pleasure." That's the kind of man he was from day one. Though it would be a mistake to take his kindness as weakness. He was definitely not a pushover. When the situation asked for it, he could be tough, even ferocious. Because that's what life calls for—otherwise you're imbalanced, and people use you.

Eventually the two Cubans, Willy and I, established a reputation. Due to his intelligence with people and his generosity, Falcon got the name The Governor, and I became The Mayor. We were two operators working from the cell, like it was a government office. Our reputation was such that inmates trusted us.

Not only did he help inmates financially, but he took the lead in putting together baseball teams so we had an outlet for all our pent up energy. Even though those games caused the odd scuffle, they were great for our morale. If you're going to cage testosterone filled men in a confined space, wouldn't you want to find a way to diffuse all of their aggression, have it channeled in a healthy direction? That would not only benefit us– the inmates, but the COs and the system as a whole. Why not find ways to diffuse conflict and create an atmosphere where people are not always at each other's throats? Often, it seemed like the goal was the complete opposite, like they wanted us knifing and preying on each other.

The average person might think that's okay. We should pay that price as we created violence and mayhem in our communities. But as I've seen and experienced, you can't put us behind bars and simply ignore us. For everyone except the lifers, there is a date set for our release. Most of us will reenter society, and will need to find our way. Wouldn't you want us to have some hope, to get the best restart possible? If your answer is no, and you think because of our crimes or our past that we should be treated like stray dogs for the rest of our existence, then many of us will come back into our communities, and pick up right where we left off. And the cycle of mayhem, violence and incarceration continues. As I mentioned in the introduction, that's the story of three out of four inmates. No, we can't reform everyone, but as I see it, the rate of recidivism tells us of a huge failure in our society and within the prison system. I truly believe we have to do better as a whole.

In the end, Falcon was doing his part, trying to make things a bit more bearable behind bars. We were on a good four year run as bunkmates, but if you hadn't noticed by now, prison can be an especially unpredictable place.

If I had lulled myself into thinking that I was going to coast to my freedom with Falcon at the wheel, and me in the passenger's seat, I was dead wrong.

What started as a dispute between two rival gangs, soon turned into a war. Willy and I were not directly involved, but we got the majority of the blame for the war and off we went to the box. As I said, prison is unpredictable and life changes at the blink of an eye.

For supposedly masterminding the conflict, both Willy and I got two years in solitary.

Falcon was sent to a different prison, and just like that, our time together was over. It was the last time I ever saw him.

I did the two years and was sent to Allenwood to serve the last three years of my sentence. It was there that the true preparation for my release began. To get my body in shape, I started to workout more seriously. I did the same for my mind.

The one thing they help you get in the federal system, if you don't already have it, is your GED. I attended classes, and since I could already read and write, unlike many other prisoners, I got one of the highest scores on my testing.

My two decades were coming to a close and I was about to be sent out into a world I no longer knew or recognized. I knew I needed to somehow find a way to support myself that didn't involve my old trade. This would not be an easy task since everything in my life up to that point involved the streets and the people in it. Almost everyone I knew, without exception, was either in prison or up to things that would probably put them behind bars. I did not have friends in high places, and no clear path forward.

I was about to be faced with the test of a lifetime.

CHAPTER ELEVEN

I WAS RELEASED FROM federal custody on August 23rd, 2011. My mother and sister came to Allenwood to pick me up. Of all places, while in prison, I had been dreaming about going to IHOP. That's the first place they took me to when I was finally granted back my freedom. We've all heard of a prisoner's last meal on death row, but no one talks about the first meal upon release. That stack of pancakes and a cup of coffee was one of the most satisfying and memorable meals of my life.

After eating we made the three-hour drive east to the Bronx and went straight to my mother's apartment. Once we were settled in, something inexplicable happened. The ground started to shake. At first, I thought that maybe my first taste of freedom in twenty years had made me dizzy, but then I saw that everyone felt it. A rare earthquake had struck New York, and not just any shaker, this one registered 5.3 on the Richter scale. The way I deemed it, I had come back into the world with a bang.

I had until six that evening to report to the halfway house where I was assigned, so I was able to spend the afternoon with my family. My mother had relocated to another part of the Bronx, which was a good thing. But unfortunately, the halfway house was back in the hood.

Once I was there, the buzz of freedom wore off fast. What I was now up against felt overwhelming. Here I was, having spent much of my youth and all of my adult years behind bars. I had my GED, but not much else– no real skills or job experience to offer the world. But I knew I needed to find a way. What other choice did I have?

The true struggle was now beginning and I was faced with some of my worst fears. As bad as prison got, no matter what you did, you always had a roof over your head and food to eat. Outside that was not the case. The most I had was my sixty days in the halfway house, after which I would need to find my own housing.

This is exactly why the majority of ex-cons end up back in the system. They fall back on what they know, their old friends, their old habits and get sucked back into the life they lived before serving time. I had promised myself that would not be me. The one thing I had, despite my deficiencies, was focus and determination. The will to overcome my situation, as hard as it was.

My work was cut out for me. I needed a job and reached out to a fellow inmate, Danny, who had also been released and told him about my situation. He said to go see his brother Gary down on a construction site on W. 36th St. in the city. When I went down there Gary offered me what he could, part-time work at close to minimum wage. It wasn't ideal but it was something. So I started taking the long train ride into the city to the job site. It was construction work, hard core manual labor, moving dirt, busting up concrete. It was brutal. I would take the train back after a full day, my hair, clothes, even the creases in my skin full of grit and dirt. I was literally building myself from the ground up at the age of thirty-eight. At the time there was a popular rap song that mentioned something about being forty and broke, and I couldn't get it out of my head. I didn't want that to be me, no way, it couldn't be.

Having been removed from society since 1992, I had missed out on the major development in the everyday use of cell phones. It was a strange experience to come out of my prison cocoon, a sort of time capsule, and see everyone's neck all crooked, locked onto their screens, while others tuned out the world, listening to music streaming through their earbuds. It really hit me how tuned out people were when I tried to get their attention and was completely ignored. Sometimes this felt like a movie too, but of the zombie genre.

There were many days when I went all the way to the job site in the city and was told there was no work. I returned the next day hoping for the best. Some days I worked, others I didn't. I was bringing in two, three hundred dollars a week. Honest money, yes, but nothing that could pay for my own apartment, let alone sustain a life. The halfway house I was assigned to being in the heart of the hood didn't help matters one bit, either.

If you've never been to the South Bronx, you wouldn't know how noisy and chaotic it is on a daily basis. There's the people hanging around every street corner, including hookers, dealers and addicts, paired with the Spanish speaking preachers who scream through with their loudspeakers for all to be saved from sin and hell.

"Ven aqui y salvate, salvate!"

You could expect to hear that sort of chaos just during the day. When night falls, the real action begins as more people congregate on the streets, while the rest of productive society retires for the evening. The sound of gunshots ringing out in the night is as normal as birdsong in the forest. What a place to live!

These are the kind of circumstances that breed desperation, the underlying emotion of those that live the life of the streets. I needed to get the upper hand in something, as this part time stuff just wasn't cutting it. That's when I ran into an old friend from the hood.

Lenny knew about my reputation, the fact I was connected with a lot of people– people from my old life, that is. He was looking for a good connection to move product and offered me a flat fee to make it happen. At the very least, I've always been a make it happen kind of guy.

I told myself I'd be the middleman, that's all. Connect the two players, take my cut, and that would be the end of it. My justification? I needed cash, bottom line. One deal would make me as much as a month of part-time work on the construction site. One deal and out.

I set Lenny up. My dealer contact, let's call him Abe, fronted him some product to be repaid by a percentage of the profits. The problem? Lenny later said he got robbed, and Abe was out five grand. In my mind the burden rested on me, since I made the introduction.

In reality, even though Lenny promised to raise the money, I was on the hook for all of it. As my previous storytelling should tell you, when you owe money to someone on the streets, it needs to be paid. This was not normal society. No cops or lawyers would get involved to negotiate a solution. It's understood that if it comes down to it, the barrel end of a gun would have the final say.

Now it was time for regret. What had I done to myself? I was overcome with a feeling of complete disgust.

I had come all this way, two decades of the prime years of my life burned away in prison, all that time, all I had put myself through, all I put my mother and father through. Shouldn't I have learned the lesson by now? Didn't Willy Falcon tell me to leave the life of the streets, to reach up not down, to forget about the hood?

The thoughts churned in me and cut me up like a meat grinder. Was I destined to live and die by the streets? Would that be my only legacy? Would my mother ever see the true me, the one inside who I knew was capable of so much more than being an ex-con with a sad and ugly history?

I met back up with Abe to learn of my fate, to see what we could work out.

"Your man Lenny left me in the hole," he said.

I apologized; told him I'd find a way to get him his money.

"That bridge is burned," he said. "You know I can't work with your guy anymore."

"I understand. I don't expect you to."

"And it doesn't change the fact that I'm five racks short."

"Let me talk to him, work it out. We'll get you the money. You know I'm good for it."

"One mistake Will... it can lead to a lot of pain."

"The pain you give, is the pain you receive."

"I like that," Abe said, an amused grin appearing on his face. "Who said it?"

"I just did."

"Those your words?"

I looked at him, gave a slight nod of my head.

"I just want to be done with this man. I did my time. What do I need to do to make this right?" I said.

His eyes fell on me. He stared for an uncomfortably long moment. Then he said something that completely took me by surprise.

"You know what... forget about it."

"You and I both know nothing is forgotten in the hood."

"I'm telling you, this one's on me Will. It's got nothing to do with you."

In that moment one thing broke, and another clicked. All my disgust had come to a head,

the years of living the same life, thinking the same way, doing the same thing, putting myself in these same situations which perpetuated the same cycle all over again. In that moment I knew I had been given my chance, probably my last chance to finally release myself from the street life that had me in its tight grip since I was a child. It was a feeling of rebirth. A real second chance, and I wasn't going to let it go to waste. Everything had led to that instant, such as in a movie, like The Matrix. Suddenly the action freezes, and the choice of the hero will decide his fate. In that moment I would seal my own destiny by finally saying goodbye to my old life. Right then and there, I told myself I would get out of the hood for good.

From then on, more things began to click. I started going down to the construction site on W. 36th in Manhattan early in the morning regardless if I had work or not. I wanted to show them I was eager, willing and able. It paid off. Little by little, I got more hours. With the extra income I was able to get my own one-bedroom apartment outside my hood. I found a girlfriend. Gary, my direct boss, encouraged me to learn the business. I was putting in long, hard days, sometimes up to fourteen hours. After a long day's work, I had another hour to commute back home on the train. None of it was easy, but I didn't mind. I was willing to do anything, wake up at any hour and work through the night, if it meant improving my life situation.

I also put my street hustling skills to work, but in a positive direction. While working my job I noticed we sent our people out to buy our work crews drinks throughout the day. We were paying two or three dollars for energy drinks, like Monster and Gatorade. This wasn't just a few people; I'm talking forty or fifty hard working men who needed hydration. With my hustling expertise, I had the thought of bringing my own cooler, buying the drinks myself, and taking the profits that would otherwise go off site.

My efforts paid off. Products sold fast. Not only was I able to make a good profit for myself, but everyone was happy. I sold the drinks cheaper than anywhere else, which meant my fellow workers got a break, and the company loved the new set up because it meant they didn't have to send workers off site during valuable time better spent on the job site. As they say, it was a win-win for everyone.

It wasn't just Gary who noticed my maniacal dedication to my work. My work ethic attracted the attention of the owner of the company, Mike Falco, who later became my second mentor.

"You have any kind of education?" he asked me one day. "I need someone who understands the numbers, can take care of some office work?"

"Of course," I told the boss. "I went to college." With that, he gave me a promotion and new responsibilities. That meant less labor and more paperwork, fine by me. As I said, I was willing to do anything to move up. For the first time, I was awarded a salary instead of an hourly wage. This made all of the difference and gave me a huge confidence boost.

I dialed that job in and Falco, the boss, came to me again. I had been moved from the construction site, to our concrete plant at this point.

"We need to find a batcher," he told me. "The guy we have is going to be leaving us."

What he didn't know was that I was observing the batcher the whole time, learning what his job consisted of. Gary and Falco did tell me to learn as much as I could about the business.

"I can batch," I said.

Falco was skeptical, and rightfully so. He had no idea the person he was working with at this point in time, and I was intent on showing him what I was capable of. That's exactly what he wanted.

"Show me," he said, as he stood over me in the tower overlooking the concrete plant.

I got on the mic and gave the orders, told the driver below to back up to the hopper.

"Rotate your barrel," I said into the microphone once he was in position.

Then I got the order and input it into the computer system which triggered the raw material that makes concrete—water, gravel, sand, cement—to drop through the hopper into the truck barrel. It went off without a glitch. Falco was impressed. I got another order, and I took care of that as well. The truth was I worked in the same area as the batcher and learned through watching his every move on the computer system that he used.

I was offered the job. I told Falco he didn't need to replace my old position, that I'd do the job of two men. We negotiated a deal with mutual benefits– I'd get a substantial pay raise, while he would save money by not having to pay the salaries of two full-time employees. But while I solved one problem—cash flow—I created a new one. My work week was now sixty to seventy hours, but it was a problem I was willing to have. For the first time, I could help my mother out financially and finally be the man I knew I could be, and build a life for myself. This gave me even more fuel, more purpose. All of that extra energy, every bit of extra fire, I applied back into my work.

CHAPTER TWELVE

SINCE MY RELEASE in 2011, each year and onward I saw my life improve. I was moving up in the company, making more money, and I even found myself in a relationship with a great woman. Maria needs to be given her due. She's the one who helped transition me back into society. She taught me about phones and the internet, since being in my prison cocoon I had missed a lot of the advances in these technologies.

She also helped in getting my driver's license and my first car. We lasted four good years, before I was reintroduced to my true love, which again proved to me that there's an invisible hand guiding my life.

If you recall, during the turmoil of my teenage years, I had a girlfriend by my side. She experienced so much of the trouble of those years. When I got busted at five in the morning at my parents' place for skipping bail, she was right there, sleeping beside me on the bed. She stayed with me through some of the worst of it, as I was in and out of prison. She kept up the vigil of prison visits for a few years, up until I got my nine year sentence. I didn't expect her to wait out my state sentence. Let's not forget how young we were. Eventually we lost touch and she moved on with her life as would be expected.

It wasn't until 2015 that I decided to reach out to her again, sending her a message on Facebook, of all places. It was a happy surprise when I got a message back. We agreed to meet in person, and the feelings I had for Aracelis were immediately reignited. In fact, they had never left, and it seemed like the feelings were mutual. I found out that she was divorced and had a daughter from that marriage.

As a result of our history together and our rekindled love, things moved quickly. I was reintroduced to her parents and showed them that I was a changed man, working for a successful construction company. I have to admit, it was with some pride that I showed them pictures of the work we did putting up buildings in the city.

They had seen what I had brought myself to as a teenager, and urged me to leave that life. Since Aracelis and I were back together, it must have been a relief to them to see how I had changed. And so it was with their blessing that I moved into Aracelis's house.

This was the one part of my old life with which I was happy to be reunited. It wouldn't be long before we were married, and continue to be till this day. In addition to this rekindled love, I received another huge blessing– her daughter Ocean became my daughter. This gave me even more purpose, a family of my own. Piece by piece my life was coming together, the broken fragments were sewing themselves into a whole, into something that made sense. A whole new Will was making himself known. That old character who spent twenty years in prison, was taking on a new role. He may have sounded the same in passing, maybe from the outside you could recognize some features. But overall, he had become a completely different man. Even my parole officer took notice.

"Spread the word," he told me. "You're doing great. People need to hear your story. It will give them inspiration."

People still had their doubts though. Especially those closest to me, my sisters. I heard about it through my mother. Unfortunately, they were planting seeds of doubt in her mind as to how things would turn out for me. They spoke as if they had a say in my destiny.

How did I react? By pushing myself even harder. Everyday I was more single minded in my focus. But still, my sisters' attitude stung.

I told my mother, and vowed to her that I would build my life to even greater heights. I was on a mission to make her proud. Much of what was driving me was my mother. I created so much pain in her life, my mission now was to shine for her. I wanted to show her what I could do, what her son was capable of. I was after redemption and I used everything, even people's doubt as fuel to accomplish that goal.

Now that I was in a position to do so, that mission also meant helping others. I knew first hand how tough it was for inmates to get back on their feet once released. Even the basics weren't a given. A couple of hundred dollars could make a world of difference for buying essentials like shoes and clothes. So when I found out old friends were returning from prison, even though I wasn't going to get mixed up with the old life, I helped more than a few buy what they needed and gave them an opportunity to work for our company. Some worked out, others didn't. But you know what they say about leading a horse to water. The best you can do is give someone a shot, the rest is up to them.

In 2016, at the urging of our owner Mike Falco, I was able to get a professional license which drastically increased my income and my professional responsibilities. Remember what my cell mate Willy Falcon said about reaching up, not down. He told me I need to get connected to the right people, those who could help raise me up. I had followed through on his advice, and had put myself in a place where I could be raised up, quite literally.

Here I was, helping lead men and run a successful super structure business. This part of my movie had some obvious metaphors. Our company's job, in which I have played a vital role, is to build skyscrapers. I had gone from the darkest of places, the dungeon of existence, and floor by floor, I have moved myself up. Instead of being a victim of my own madness, my actions after leaving prison led me to better and better places. All because I gave myself a chance.

Once I got my professional license, which required a minimum of five years working in the field, things really began to take off. As I mentioned, I shot up to a different income category. That gave me more options, and I needed them to figure out our living situation.

The house I was living in with Aracelis was nice, but right back in the hood. The problem was people knew where I was, and it wasn't necessarily people with whom I wanted to associate with again.

One night there was a knock at the door. When I opened it, Billy came walking through it, a character from the old days. He may not have known or recognized it, but the Will that was before him was a completely transformed character. The issue was it looked as if he had stayed the same. When a person stops evolving, they may assume that you have as well. If that assumption is unfounded, as it was in this case, those two people who at one time were connected in the past, cannot recreate what once was—because in reality, it doesn't exist anymore.

Billy's arrival made me uncomfortable. For one, it was nine in the evening, around the time to make my way to get some rest and prepare for the next day. That's what having a future, a tomorrow is all about—you need to be in shape for tomorrow, because tomorrow has demands.

I could see Billy was hard up. Reluctantly, I spent some time with him and then sent him on his way with a few dollars. I didn't like how someone could surprise us with a visit, and at such a late hour at that. Especially someone who had been tangled up in the street life, and by the looks of it, still was. After that day Aracelis and I made the decision to sell her house and leave the Bronx altogether.

We got rolling on the moving plans right away. The first thing we did was get some workers in to fix the place up. In less than a month we had the house on the market. The bigger task was finding a place to move into. We knew we didn't want to stay in the five boroughs, so we focused our search on counties within driving distance of the city.

We were looking for the right house and neighborhood, but just as important, it needed to be close to a good school for our daughter. After looking at a few houses, we found one in Rockland County that met all of our desired criteria.

When I was first released in 2011 and was living in the halfway house with barely a hundred bucks to my name, my mother reminded me of my situation. In Spanish she said I would have to find a way to get on my feet, and reminded me that I couldn't rely on anyone but myself. Not even my sisters.

"They won't even give you a couch anymore," she told me. I must have sounded like a madman when I said to her with great bravado, "You wait. I'm gonna have five couches and when I do, you can tell them they can come over and stay with me."

Sometimes you need to speak the words so someone else can hear them, no matter how crazy they sound. It doesn't matter if no one else believes them, because all that matters is that you do. But believing is not enough. Any lunatic can devise a scheme and scream it out to the world. Once you have that vision, you need to go and get it.

Walking into that house in Rockland County, seeing the layout and the backyard with the pool, we knew it was the one. But it wasn't until I was sitting in a lawyer's office, signing the paperwork with the confidence of a loan secured in my name that it was made real. I would be moving into my dream house. Just as I told my mother eight years prior. They weren't just words, I had made it happen. It was both surreal and very satisfying.

With this move we could also take our daughter Ocean out of her inner-city school in the South Bronx and put her into a private school. That meant going from a crowded classroom of thirty plus kids per teacher, to having a teacher for every six or seven students. When we saw how rapidly she progressed in this new environment, we realized what a blessing this move was to our family. Ocean went from an introverted kid who struggled with reading and writing, to someone who exuded confidence in and out of the classroom.

In 2018 we discovered that my mother had pancreatic cancer. She would live for two more years, long enough to see what I accomplished. The promise I had made to her was fulfilled. The house was a kind of marker, a threshold that showed me, and others, how far I had come.

In the eight years I had been released I had gone from being an ex-con with a GED and living in a halfway house, to living in my dream house, working in a field that built things up, rather than destroyed them.

My story began in the streets. The twelve-year-old kid who sent bricks designed to build things smashing through car windows and then lit those cars on fire. We burned down cars, but also businesses and ultimately lives, including our own. When I chose a different path, time contracted and I reeled in the dream that I saw on the horizon, as bright as the burning sun. At least I was able to give that to myself, my family, and my mother before she took her last breath.

She could pass away, knowing I would be okay. She could pass away, as I wanted her to, a proud mother of a redeemed son.

CHAPTER THIRTEEN

THE REASON FOR sharing my story is so that you can see yourself in me. With everything against me– my own history, the obstacles and inner doubt, I pulled myself out of hell. To say that no one gave me anything is a lie. I was given a chance, and I took it. In fact, I was given several chances by many, including the law, Aracelis, and my parents. I survived more fights than I can remember, multiple stabbings, and I was shot in the back. It took me years and many hard lessons to realize that at some point, I needed to take one of those opportunities and run with it. If you don't do that, you don't have any hope at all. That's why people fall back into their old life, their old habits. It can happen to anyone, not just ex-prisoners like me. You don't need to ever see the inside of a concrete cell under the watch of indifferent COs to create your own special kind of hell.

No doubt, life is a complicated game. I'm sure you don't need me to tell you that. But the least any of us can do is hold tight to what I told myself through the worst of times– give yourself a chance, a shot. And keep giving yourself that chance.

With that said, I want to share another saying that's been very effective, coined by yours truly– The Blessing Run Downhill.

What I mean by this is once you're blessed, it's up to you to share those blessings so others can be touched by them. That's what life is all about. If you live your life this way, then maybe you can make something out of your pain other than thick scars. Maybe you can leap over it, transcend it, and achieve such heights that others will see you as a shining example, and you can turn around and help them do the same.

First you lift yourself up, then those closest to you, and then maybe you can touch even more lives. In this way your blessings run downhill, build momentum, and envelop everything and everyone, especially those trying to pull themselves up to a higher place.

I was sent away for a good part of my youth and for many of the prime years of my adulthood for crimes I committed before I was twenty-one. This is no excuse, but a fact. I was a kid at the time my crimes were committed. I had veered off in a terrible direction and paid the highest price anyone can pay, except for losing their life. Time lost.

It's true, I was given many chances to reform by the system and by my parents. But I refused them. I was pushed by an inner mania that took two decades to work out of my system. It pains me till this day to know that someone's life ended because of my actions. A friend's life, at that. As a result I was doled out a penalty which my society demanded. I did that time. Regardless, I cannot raise the dead. I cannot turn back the clock and undo what my hands have done. All I can do now is ask my creator for forgiveness, and do everything I can to wash away my sins even though that's impossible. At the same time, there are many things I did do right despite my past, and it's those things I hope you can take to help you on your life journey.

First of all, life makes no promises. As you have read, mine has been a path of blood, sweat and tears. No one owes you anything. Everything must be earned. The reality is, your only guarantee is to wake up every day and to struggle.

I gave everything to the streets. When I was released, I gave that same energy to my own life, to my own expansion, and to my family. That includes my deceased mother and father.

As I mentioned at the beginning, three out of every four inmates ends up back in jail. That's a horrible statistic and it doesn't need to be that way. I'm here to shine a light on that reality and because I hope to help in changing it. As has been said before and will continue to be said, in order to make a big change, you need to first be willing. I know some people just won't change and that's okay. People may not want you to change, either. I've lost friends over my life as a changed man.

In order for me to get ahead I had to change. Not necessarily who I was at the core, but I had to change my ways of being and doing. I needed to find a better system that could improve my life, because my old ways were broken. If those around me didn't want to come along for the ride, so be it. At least I know where I'm headed, and I know there's others like me I'll find along the way.

People who know they can do better, who feel like I did all along, like you have potential, a higher calling—you can and you must go for the best in yourself. That's the first step. Like a player in Vegas with a royal flush, you've got to push every last chip into the pile. You've got to go all chips in on yourself. And here's the thing I learned. Recall how many times I had done wrong and gone wrong and still I gave myself a chance? From it, I learned that unlike Vegas, if you do go all chips in– not into the criminal life, but into life improvement– you can never go bust. That's right. When you actually bet on yourself, you have an endless supply of chips, of chances, of opportunities. If one thing doesn't work out, something else eventually will, that is if you keep going all in. That's the secret. The power lives inside of me, and inside of you is an endless well. It's called energy, life, spirit, whatever word you want to call it. And with that, you can make anything happen.

Be real. Stay strong.

And most of all, give yourself a chance.

AFTERWORD

HERE'S A HARD truth I've learned over years. No matter what someone else has accomplished in their life, they can't tell you exactly what to do in order to improve your situation, assuming that's what you want. I truly believe the best they can do is to share their story, and let you take from it what you will. Sure, there are some basic principles that can help light the way. But beyond that, it's up to you. There is no single blueprint, for the very fact that we're all different. Not only is our individual situation unique, but so are our goals, aspirations and talents. What that means is that your path will inevitably be different than mine. That is both a great challenge and a blessing.

The challenge is that if you're like me and you lived the majority of your existence in prison, you must not deceive yourself into believing that once you get out into society, you can get right back to where you left off. If this is your thought process or how you feel, you probably need to change in some ways. Change is very difficult, and the transition to life on the outside will most likely be slow, full of obstacles and temptations. There will be times where it seems everything is against you, and you must resist the urge to give up or to play the victim.

If there's one thing I can pass on it's that with opportunity comes responsibility. As you've read I was given those chances, but it wasn't until I responded with everything I had, that my life began to improve. That's the meaning of responsibility– the ability to respond. Only then did I gain the upper hand and get out of sheer survival mode. That really is the first step, and it cannot be skipped. In other words, if I wasn't willing to work long hours and give all that I had when I got out, I wouldn't be where I am today. If I caved in to my worst urges, I would probably be yet another statistic.

The blessing in that is that your path will not be anyone else's but your own, full of unforeseen surprises and gifts. I had no idea that by showing up at the construction site and busting concrete I would eventually get the attention of those who could lift me higher. At each turn I was given more responsibility, and I ran with it. It's like the parable of the sower. Once the seeds are sown they take time to grow roots. All I did was stay the course and kept watering, even when things looked bleak. Then the right people came into my life. I was reintroduced to my old girlfriend, who later became my wife. But not until I was turning the corner, becoming a new man. I had no idea I would be gifted a daughter, either. Really, it's been one blessing after another and that's the beauty of life. Despite the difficulty, when you start to make the right moves, unexpected blessings and opportunities follow. It's what makes living worthwhile.

Don't expect things to go exactly as they did for me. That would be unrealistic. Your story is yours, not mine. I told you mine so you would give yourself a chance to write your own– and I hope you make it something epic.

Never forget, to make it epic and be the hero of your own story, you've got to give yourself a chance. So do that—give yourself that chance. You may be surprised, even shocked by what you can accomplish. I certainly have been.

NOTES

Printed in the USA
CPSIA information can be obtained
at www.ICGtesting.com
LVHW051822080823
754668LV00014B/1529

9 798987 123409